VIA Folios 162

The Bronx Unbound
OVVERO I VERSI BRONXESI

THE BRONX UNBOUND

OVVERO I VERSI BRONXESI

Poems by Angelo Zeolla

BORDIGHERA PRESS

All rights reserved. Parts of this book may be reprinted only by written permission from the author, and may not be reproduced for publication in book, magazine, or electronic media of any kind, except in quotations for purposes of literary reviews by critics.

© 2023, Angelo Zeolla

Library of Congress Control Number: 2023940260

Published by
BORDIGHERA PRESS
John D. Calandra Italian American Institute
25 W. 43rd Street, 17th Floor
New York, NY 10036

VIA Folios 162
ISBN 978-1-59954-195-2

Table of Contents

Where are the Real Italians?	9
Tamarro	16
Sidewalk Reality	22
Guido Poet	24
Neapolitan Cigarettes	29
Colle Sannita Poetry	31
Mondrayork	34
Crazy Annie	36
Stoop Dub	38
Pezzo Da Novanta	41
A New York	50
Guido Poetics	52
New Haven	56
Sub Terrain 6 Train Blues	59
Joey's Footnote	61
XTC	65
After September 11th	66
Spiritual Crisis	69
Maddalena	71
La nubiana ritrovata	74
Guido Haiku	80
La Resistenza	82
ACKNOWLEDGMENTS	87
ABOUT THE AUTHOR	89

Where Are the Real Italians?

[1]

Pizzeria burned down,
Newspaper reads: reasons
unknown.

Giuseppe sits in his dark apartment,   He's
home alone.
Stares intensely at the picture of *Nonno*   on
the wall,

In a gilded frame suspended
by a rusty nail   he plunged
through so it would not fall
and shatter into little pieces
that would lodge under foot.

The black and white photo stares back.
Eyes brimming with the hope of the
next life,
Face worn out like Giuseppe's, but
Nonno didn't do no dope.

*A dò stanno i suoi amici?   Sono
spariti nella sera cercando quel
tesoro di paradiso.*

Runs his fingers through his hair
all that greasy mess. Confesses
his sins aloud,
acts out a scene to that film:
       You Talking to me?

Cuz I got an offer you can't refuse.
Live and lose.
Eat or be eaten.
Come back you dumb Guinea or
you'll catch a beatin!

But They were devoured,
devoid of their culture
their cadavers rotted
as the vultures circled

souls risen but gone forever,
gazed at the picture of *Nonno,*
Once more, faded just a bit.

[2]

Memories die man!
Peppino's sick o' that shit!

Takes a sip of the juice calms
him down just a bit.
It's a trip.
Volare nel blu dipinto di blu.

Turns on the tube,
Pacino is on! Serpico
he's that cop, right?

De Niro, Raging Bull,
That La Motta could fight.

Right!?!?!
Peppy he's that dumb Dago losin'

his temper.
The Wop slingin' the Pasta.
He fights with a knife.
Stabbed his brother for
fuckin' his wife.
That's life.
What can he say or do but
ask the question:
Where are the Real Italians?

Mandolins sound!
Soil plowed with the peasant's blood.
Such hallowed ground,
Clothes sewn with the red thread to
ward off the evil eye.

Where was it when they hit Ellis Island?

Giuseppe quietly asks coming down from the
mental cloud he rides.

Confides to the heavens,
asks for advice,   and
wishes soon to converse with angels.

As a young boy Joe
studied Italian
never could get the accent straight
more Guido than Guinea

[3]

hated when   The Zips

called him *R'O' Mericano*

He always wanted to be
Un Italiano Vero.

Months changed and Years passed
had to make that cash fast, with high
school done he found a job
on the street where
numbers were run.

He lowered himself to
a lowly miser.
Scraped up enough dough
to go to the other side, the
Old Country.

On his arrival survival
ceased,
Joe was just another tourist,
an outsider from the inside.

Sands of time turned to glass it
shattered
and lodged itself under foot
shooting pain up to his brain
causing blood curdling screams of:

WHERE ARE THE REAL EYETALIANS?

Rolls a joint, takes a puff of
the Buddha seed
He's trippin' off some Jamaican weed.

Looked at *Nonno*'s picture once more.

Dulled eyes   still visible
but no more face worn out without the use of dope.

He's flippin' like a staggerin' wino
and starts buggin' out, seein' these
apparitions and shit!

Clemenza's got gun in hand.

[4]

Tommy's got the power to amuse also a
short fuse.

Marty finds his pleasure in
devouring mamma's lasagna.

He hears Chico Marx
speakin' in that broken English/broken Italian,
as il Bambino falls asleep over that poppy seed *papavero*.

Looks at the picture once more, no eyes
filled with hope nor face worn out not by
the usage of dope.

A cold hush fills the room
as the frame falls through the air the rusty nail
could no longer bear the weight it
had borne for all those years.

Pascal's poetry was bold.

DiDonato's Christ was buried in concrete for
tasting a forbidden fruit so sweet.

Electricity flowed through the air as
Sacco and Vanzetti burned slow.

And where are you Carlo Tresca
on this damp night?
Where are you Joe Petrosino?
Rotting in Palermo's alleyways?

Behold the olive skinned black haired   beauty
corrupted by blond dye
        and blue contacts in eyes.

There was never a deeper stare
than those of her black opaque eyes.   There was
never a sight so fair, as the shattered glass from
the frame lay scattered over a blur that once
was a vision that told of a thousand hardships
and triumphs.

In robe and bare feet, of
reality he was no longer
aware

[5]

as his feet planted themselves
on the fragments of glass an
epiphany revealed itself to
him in his high mass.

It faded slowly to show us the error
of our ways. But the days are long

gone and persecution would no
longer last and we would make that
money fast
losing ourselves in all that
success, leaving our
descendants to cope with all
such distress, brought upon
them by the question of:

Where are the Real Italians?

And he peered down to his feet as
the floor ran red with his blood his
body slowly crumbled his last
words he barely mumbled:

Shards, so many little shards, and so light—
where do I fit into the starry night?

Tamarro

Today
I was
minding my
own business

posted up on the
corner of
Roberts and
Crosby   Aves
bearing   witness
to the heavenly
donzelle
who floating by
leave the scent of designer
perfumes in their
delicate wake

giving the daily
panorama
that little
something   that
negates the
simplicity inherent
to the daily
routine of the
come and go
sparking it in a
sublime that
drenches
everything in a
magnificence

none other than
her inherent
grace.

Limping along in that
get up you tried to
save face in some
half ass
gallo strut
talking shit and
staring down
this bard
so hard it was drastic

Alla fine:

si nu guapp 'e cartone!

your steez is plastic
 so I'd suggest you hire a bodyguard
so you won't suffer the humiliation of looking spastic,
in front of these neighborhood girls that pass,
by my debasing you poetically rather than stomping
a mud hole in that ass:
my verse is like a *strega*'s curse
that sends you to Mass
to light candles confess your sins
and fill collection plates
with shit loads of cash so you can start fresh
with a clean slate
in hopes of avoiding a sucker's fate.

But not even a million
Dollars in the Vatican Bank
could absolve you

Of your *tamarrità*

There's something about
Your dove-swoon swagger
That makes the record skip

You know like when
wise guys flip because
it dawned on them
that The Life
was just *"merd ra gent"*

Ué frate', me sient'?

Your gear summed up:

Shades *da fighetto:*
Check!

*A' Maglietta su cui
C'è scritto* "ITALIAN MADE":
Check!

Typical
charcoal colored jeans with that fresh belt
from Armani Exchange finished off by those white
rebooks
So fresh that They even glisten in the shade:
Check!

Now let me guess,
Amic'-----
your Grand Parents
were

born down on Morris Ave
Great Grand Parents were
probably *Tamarri di
Periferia*, that came
over and told the
future generations
that they were from
Palermo to
avoid that *tu vuo'
Fa' l'Americano* Confusion.

Tamarro, I ain't
mad at you for reppin'
Sicily even tho you
don't speak a damn
word of *Palermitano*.

I won't even fault you For
the *tricolore* tattoo of Sicily
on your right bicep that you
flex
pumping
fist in air singing
"SONO UN ITALIANO"

It's all that chest
puffing and posing
where   you're as
believable As James Caan in the
Godfather exclaiming
STRUNZ with a Yiddish accent
That bothers the shit out of me

So I must call out the
idiocy in purveying

yourself as the poster-
boy for guys like me
who walk these
neighborhood blocks
as tho they were the
same *vicoletti* their
immigrant forefathers
bid farewell to walking
the moon lit country
roads glorious in their
sweet simplicity.

Guys like me
who can't
hang their Ethnic
Intricacies in a closet
like FILA jumpsuits
After trippin' balls on
XTC
Down in the trance room
At Webster Hall

Guys like me
Caught in between
Societies of Socrates and
Dionysus.

Who write poetry
With the scope Of making sense of
this whole
"who am I" mess
by jumping desks

Anomalies
For which

Resolutions
remain to be seen

who fiend
for cut and dry solutions
to this
Saturday night fever stress

Because *tutto sommato*
You're just *Tamarro*
Nothing   more
Nothing less.

The concrete is always
cleaner
on your side of the Street
I guess.

Sidewalk Reality

I usually tend to associate with weirdoes, winos,
whores, wise-asses, and wannabes,
kind of like the street's five w's:

Even beneath all that refuse there still lays the saga of broken
spirits.

Losers in my book are winners that never succumbed to the
pangs of the herd.

In the night I see humanity: Lil' Joe
smacks his shit up in front of the
Church, needles litter the streets and he
flies like my *makature* flapping in the
midnight wind.

His high daze gives him sights of black
haired beauties that have feline features
and devil eyes.

A dò sta mia regina! He cries.

And then there's Maria with her goods.
Her mother sold her body, fate written before   pen
hit page.

Now she turns tricks to feed her kids.
Gets pummeled by her *magnaccio* if
she doesn't make her cut.

Wise *barbone* let me take a sip from

your brown bag flask so I may drown
my sorrows.

My jaw tenses as I see a group of ravers x-ed the
fuck out sharing love that is always lost on these
streets.

Guido Poet

The *cedesmer nera* growls
Speeding down the Hutchinson River Parkway
Freestyle songs set the symphony for this lonely Night.

I'm a traveler caught between two worlds battling
to blend in like a chameleon of
Cool Water and leather over coats so that I
can quit sticking out while fitting in like a
cactus *nel deserto di Sonora.*

Essentially I'm the Guido Poet,
Not to be confused with *Guinizelli.*

I devour slices in basement pizzerias, (Louie
and Ernie's if you ask)
I don't walk, I strut down the street like
it's everybody's business.

I shed tears at tragedies sung about this chick named
Maria who was the lover of a drug dealer, who never
got to make love a reality for an admirer
that composed songs in homage to such *bellezza* scintillating &
       grandiose.

Who said a Guido can't be a Poet
(by no means to be confused with Cavalcanti) in
that fresh outfit from Armani exchange?

Stil'Novisti had the formula down:
The Poet achieved Immortality thru his
Words and was modest all the while

He forged sonnets that made Woman
An angel that gave men the privilege
To be touched by her nonchalant stare.

Fast forward to the epoch of Latin Soul
and aqua net hold: It isn't a far cry from
the days of *Beatrice* because
my Heart beats eternally for forbidden

runaway love who dressed in leather mini
and black cherry garter belts of humility
leaves guys with stifled tongues when
she's scoped, talking foul mouthed to one
of her girlfriends in front of spring time
stoop, out driver side windows,
and she bids those souls of up-the-
block gridlock, with the softness of
her thick strawberry painted lips, to
breathe and be on their fuckin' way.

Man, the streets are fodder for my stanzas
because I see paradisiacal schemes   in
manicured nails, tanning salon skin, dolce and gabbana cologne,
        velour tracksuits,
and Act 3 dreams.

Love ain't just something found in
the Courts of Kings,
it's in the neighborhood
Playgrounds where old men play *bocce* on   Courts of Sand.

I'll take Aristotle's advice and find truth in the
happy medium of two extremes, that of upper
class poetics and what's hidden between

Sergio Valente seams.

Because even if my
Compari say I'm weird in the end This
new middle world I fashion Thru
Poetry will be My Thing:
So maybe "Guido Poet" doesn't
have such a bad ring.

In my Bronx accent I recite
verse knowing that my lines
traverse realms Like subway
trains
whose rumblings sing

       the song of
sleepless city that shall
dream forever.

If my pen runs out of ink
I'll shout my Poetry
to the streets, to the
skies, to the Parks
That touch
Pelham Bay,
Prospect, and
The Battery.

And a mixture of styling mousse,
divine stanzas, And
Lil Suzy
shall inspire all insanity

inscribed on Modern sheets
of papyrus.

And I the Guido Poet shall
illuminate the third eye Searing its
iris with literary techniques and
poetic devices finding beauty
between the lines never putting one
Mask above the other because I'd
rather have a classical mess of
refinery and riff raff define my
actions than the compromise of
Self according to the tastes of
Padroni, that dole out dough of
Rationality to Poetic Peasantry from
their high horses and pass judgment
upon them like stale pieces of bread.

So like Picasso said:
"in the end we must kill our fathers."
I'm the Guido Poet

              because between
worlds I wander without
remorse for those I may
offend pondering the
idiosyncrasies of joy and pain
in my manner to no bitter end
meanwhile seeming The Fool to
the elite for what to them is a shameful blend that brings high
        society to street level.

So you can chalk this all up to
the ranting of a rebel Who may

come off a hoodlum in his
thieving of the Muse's
Harpsichord Melody like
Helen to Troy but he knows that he's
done driving down The Hutch towards his own self-determined
           disco Destiny.

Neapolitan Cigarettes

Smoking Hash down and
Out in deep summer Samnite
Alleys seated on steps of marble
Inhaling smoke between passes,
I understood that your soul
Was timeless and profound like
The fountain of youth that De Leon
Sought in vain.

And *tipa* dig the fact that no
One can tear you down because
With one wink you convert
Counts into clowns and Poof!
Castiglione's *Courtesan* Is no
longer relevant in a land
Without refinery.

Dig the fact that no body
keeps your soul because it
Was born free and shall never
Die like homes abandoned In
desperate Diaspora.

You throw me a smile that
Outshines that treasure of the sable sky
 To which serfs would recite
Prayers with the hope that some
Might fall to fruitless fields so
They'd no longer slave for
their Feudal lord.

And before we smoked this Neapolitan
Cigarette my idea of a world where a
Socratic good was possible had taken
Its final breath.
You appeared like the
Angel Gabriel to the Blessed Mother
And rekindled the flickering flame
Of hope with your sweet laugh, like Gasoline, giving
me visions of the good life.

Colle Sannita Poetry*

*written in front of Pizza MeD

Small town mother feeds her autistic adolescente seed a slice of pizza
and all I take for granted is made more apparent by this soul trapped
in his handicap since birth.

I'm seated outside taking in
This poignant scene as Paper-
dolls pass alongside marble
marciapiede, casually
looking the other way, their
highlighted dark locks flutter
in the early evening breeze.

I'm smacked from the pedestal of
 American arrogance I pose upon
fully attired in
Ralph Lauren jogging suit
white Reeboks, guinea tee,
figaro chain and golden
horn to match.

It's all illuminated like pigeons on an elevated track
to the orange halogen light bulbs of street
lanterns that stand in the hot pavement of the sweltering
summer bastard night and for once I really see my
ungrateful indiscretions.

The fact that I can walk straight,
talk straight come and go as I please,
piss and drink with ease, appreciate

life's subtleties, until that moment,
was insignificant like the pebbles
lodged in the soles of my sneakers.

Son wanders back into the cramped
and cozy pizzeria, while his mother
gossips with the
Sicilian landlady who
stands on her balcony above the doorway shouting
down to her about the discotheque theme echoing
off the ancient apartment buildings in Piazza.

Mother stands there below sipping at her Coca
Cola light digging the techno rhapsody
full of tenacity as its sound so
displeasing to *la vecchietta la' su*
eases the pain propelled by stares of
disdain directed at her from the faces
of townsmen that pass with mixed
minds of pity and relief to remind
her that her problem is just that:
Not theirs.

She takes solace that at least her son is
oblivious to the cross that the indifferent
looks of Colle Sannita. force her to bear
because his existence
reveals the

imperfections   of
this mountain town.

I grow sad for the have-nots that have not
been given the means to truly seize the day.

It's the little things that set us free like
being able to cross the street without
someone holding your hand.

To be able to play *nasconderella* without being
subjected to the worried watchful eyes of
scrutiny that take notice of everywhere you
stand.

That kitten over there cakes her face up in
make up to hide what the community has
deemed her ugly shortcoming.

And that cat over in front of the *Tabaccaio*
shouts at angels that pass cradling his
coglioni in the palm of his hand
to show his guaglioni that he's The man.

I'll just sit still and bask in the country love

                borne to earth in the blue light of a full country moon
that makes the strands of mortar that bind the cobblestone
pavement lucid like silver lining.

Realizing that my freedom to
do as I please is his freedom
of no judge, no jury, and no
worry.

Image has no sway in his court of eternal
innocence, for he can truly run free in green
fields, face brushed softly by a fresh summer
breeze, because hell bears no existence in his
ignorance.

Mondrayork

Saturday night
Ngope ru mol a Mondragone Emcees
rhyme these *versi immacolati*
defaming *cosidetti sfigati* For even
picking up a microphone,

Motorini fly by purring in the distance
and the skaters are the shit *nel stare a
mostro con i loro trick e per la strada si
vedono   passare guaglioncelle,
con quei loro sguardi da stelle,   che
vanno di moda vestite tutto chic.*

And one cat over by the kebab truck sheepishly asks another:

O Fra', ma 'a canna 'a tieni?

Other cat *si esce fore' con un pezzo*—
tipo un mattone, a fat chunk he
copped
Over *a ru terz' munn'*
Si fa sta pinta, it gets
sparked
And soon *ognuno* se
ne va
a chiedere:

Ma stu tir' se po' fa' o no?

A red moon draped in *malinconia* peeks down at
streets that stay littered con *spazzatura*

As *i caramba* drive by with
their ice grills that make
blood chill,
cioè fanno paura,

the perfume of tainted Mediterranean air lingers
thru the scene
and nocturnal writers throw up a wild style piece
that declares to new arrivals that peep every street
sign, in wonder, as they bewilderedly walk:

Benvenuti a Mondra York!

Crazy Annie

As the six train stands silent on the El,
its thunder stifled by train traffic ahead
the sidewalks nonetheless
set the stage *per lo spettacolo,*

Where Crazy Annie, The
neighborhood *Strega,*
jabbers incessantly in low
Italian
'bout how The Vatican got
us pegged for a bunch of
Jesus-bead counting
buffoons catholic school
children walk by sippin'
unpopped cherry flavored
quarter drinks oblivious to
such heresy that renders the
atmosphere electric—

And they stare *alla vecchiarella*
Seated there on milk crate throne
Con in mano un bastone Who
doesn't need four walls Because
these streets are home sweet
home where she rests her silver
lining filled sable tresses and
possesses brown eyes that bewitch
the soul with their dim shimmer
that give her an
air of human
divinity that

confesses bitter
sweet fare wells,
feste divertenti
and times faded.

"Pare na janara!",
esclama uno che la passa   e subito lo manda a
fare in culo— ella comanda la massa   poiché
nobilmente stellata

d' umiltà   manco fosse una monarca,

so show some respect or she'll
put you in check and fill your
days with *brutto figlio di*
puttana uncertainties *perché*
tuo giorno è un viaggio che
non ha ritorno.*

Thus catholic school
children pass With
hazel eyes of awe and
wonder whose
unenlightened ears
yearn to truly fathom
exchanges burned
Indelible to third eye
which spark guido
poetic strophes that
combust and cause
fuss thru-out boogie
down Buhre Ave
atmosphere.

Stoop Dub

As beads
Of sweat trickle down the
flesh of this mid-summer
night

The six train softly
Crawls down the elevated towards
Pelham Bay Station echoing
along *sogni d'oro* side street of
Mahan Ave twilight

Where wide eyed *jazzmatazz*
minded poet puffs a *toscanello*
in child-like emulation Of those
long gone
Birds of Passage

whom he struggles to remember
in black & white contemplating
their possible exploits in early
novecento Pittsburgh
on 3 in the morning front stoop

Amidst ambivalent outer-borough
Banter about M5 beamers Dark
tints and a chromed out set of
new shoes—

The moon looms overhead
Knocked for six because the
Stars won't come out and play

Cigar smoke drifts sheepishly
In the mix and guidos curse
The pungent stench it wreaks

They curse the poet decrying him
him a freak stinking of *toscanello* smoke who rocks a cheap pair
       of penguin
chuck taylors whose ideal world is one
in which all the banks are razed down
to their last glowing ember and the only
currency in circulation is that raw
poetry found at the bottom of one's
soul that causes cats to be one with the
machinery of night floating across roof
tops contemplating Bop and always
remembering that
BIRD LIVES
E BRIGANTE SE MORE!

Where one only needs to be
content with the rumble of
barreling six train
toward metropolitan
sublime infinity

Where all this neighborhood
bullshit goes up in smoke like
puffs off a freshly lit
toscanello and the
jazzmatazz minded poet is
enlightened by tumultuous
twisted metal
gallop of six train iron stallion
booking it double time for

heavenly Bleeker St.   so Dago
Bards can recite some poetry
and make eyes at doll faced
subterranean   sirens that
whisper sonnets heavenly.

Pezzo da Novanta

I.

Pezzo da novanta,
The Guido Poet
Stands before you
Head held high
A bold individual with nothing
To give you but these neighborhood verses
That roll thru this basement cafe off his
tongue with *cafone* candor kind of like
cadillacs crawling cautious
in forget about it
funeral processions as hearses haul off the cadaver of that same old
Zip to Saint Raymond's Cemetery.

You know the one you so enjoy
eulogizing to starry eyed black
dress granddaughters counting off
novenas in Our Lady of whoever
pews with those trite lines of how
he was a hard working American
who espoused family values, who
towed the party line, *che s'è fatt'*
nu cule quadrate* who never once
asked Big Brother if he was too
good to spare a dime.

Pezzo da novanta,
I had you pegged back and
Forth even before you
came prancing into The

social club the night of
little Carmine's First Communion
with your condescending air, Six
thousand dollar suit, cinematically
coiffed hair do, reeking of cheap
cologne and dead presidents wadded
over in that silver money clip you
copped at some jewelry store way
out there in South Shore,
Staten Island.

And you came traipsing
across the parquet floor With
some of that   good ol' blue
eyes elegance, Half stepping
to podium,
Wing tips all aflutter,
Manhandling the microphone (I
must say for about
a millisecond I was impressed.)

Then you cleared
your throat and
started to sputter The
same old lopsided
statistics 'bout how
we Dagos got all the
other poor
huddled masses beat,

'bout how we've lost our
gold teeth and penchant
for fig trees
in front gardens,

'bout how
We're model Americans
and maybe some of that
assimilation rag might
rub off on those
Mexicans that man the
stoves in Crosby
Pizzeria.

And while decrying the negative
depictions Relevant to Tony
Soprano While eloquently
extolling the virtue of visionary
explorer,
Giovanni da Verazzano, Giving us
your take on what a dim lit dive the
U. S. of A would Be without the
contributions of the descendants of
Ancient Rome, Regaling us with
some apocalyptic alternate
possibility had Chris

Not come over and
declared the Native
population:
Indians.

Pezzo da novanta,
you're one *Ricordatevi
di Roma* shy of sounding
like Mussolini

(Che coglione!)

And then you start the same old story
'bout how it's
all about climbing the social ladder
'bout how Bartolomeo
and Nicola were just two
poor Zips who were
victims of circumstance,
exclaiming: *If one of*
their compari
back then had let them know the political score . . .
but then again to make a *frittata* you've got to
break quite a few eggs after all every wine press
has a few dregs.

Pezzo da Novanta, The name
of your game is perseverance
and Forming new world
habits . . . .

According to you:
Va' fa mocc' with
Bilingual Education,
Because the Nuns at Saint
Anthony's Never co-opted
lily white Anglo-American
vernacular
For that soil filled slang spoken
by Siciliani e Salernitani.

Secondo te:
We owe America thanks for reminding us
day in and day out that if we kept
stepping out of line there would be a shit

load of hell to pay and look at us now
after the many trials and tribulations
lynchings and exploitation self-hatred
and assimilation until finally we wised up
and got the 'Mericano routine down
where we fail to connect the dots Never
thinking that we were once in the 21st
century greenhorn's spot because you've
got to pay a cover charge somehow
to enter in this
Studio 54 land of the free.

II.

All I have to say is:

I can't figure out
Why a Godfather watchin'
Pasta and provolone eatin' Half-ass
Ed Sullivan
Introducin' *Topo Gigio* Mangled
Neapolitan
Dialect speakin' Mario
Lanza
And Frank Sinatra
Listenin'
Who wouldn't know
what the fuck
Caruso Crooned
about even If his
words were like a
Figaro
Chain glistenin'

Off some hairy chested
Camorrista throwin'
His cold glare up and
Down *'O Vicolo* scopin'
His *comare* as she passes
young hash smokin' Emcees
that freestyle:

                                        Ti sei mai chiesto perché'???

Some misogynistic shrink seein'
Multi layered wife cheatin'
Guapp', forever retellin' his
Father's old tales of how
Beautiful the ninth ward was
Before the mulignans
Moved in and razed
whatever Virgin on
the Half shell front
yard sculpture they
could find too, Gets
you all in a tizzy
*mentre Cristoforo se
la passa liscio*   due to
historical Hypocrite
cop out
Context that makes Everything
ethnic
And sarcastically unethical.

After all, it was done under Universal
banner of the
Wondrous seafarin'
Small pox carrier hand
Cuttin' gold lustin'

Indian enslavin'
Heathen Convertin' Round
world
Maintainin'
Spanish crown
Sailin' Niña
Pinta
Ma
OOOOOOO Santa Mari'
Nata voda co' sta storia!

If you hear a Zip
Exclaimin'
Mannaggia Colombo!
It isn't so outlandish
Because he was probably
Just your run of
the mill
Genovese who
in The end
would
Have been schived
The fuck out
By those first
McKee Port coal
minin' Gold tooth
grinnin' *Braccianti*
baresi.

Immigrants and imperialists Are
opposite sides of that
sentimental scratched up Penny
that lovers find on
First date

Washington Square Park
Strolls amidst the Chess
hustlers that attempt to sucker
some unsuspectin' stoner poet
into a 15 dollar game when all
he has in his pocket is the
twenty-five cents he found by
the statue of Garibaldi where
the ghosts of organ grinders
loiter dejected
by the fact that the
monkey no longer
claps in time to that
street sweep lonely
night shift melody.

Pezzo da Novanta You'd
say I was takin' crazy
pills
But I'm the type to find More
similarities
Between Cristoforo
And Joe Colombo
Than with my immigrant
Great War
Grandfather
Wounded
Decorated
Veteran
Made American citizen
By servin' his time in Lost
generation hell.

I'll play Carlo Tresca
To your Generoso Pope
If it means not
Having to be a part of this
Whole *Bella Figura*
Farce that would have Me say *Il
settentrione* Is where the beatin'
heart of Italian America gets its
rhythm.

Pezzo da Novanta,
Your style is fugazi
*Piuttosto tamarro Ve
lo dico Chiaro:
Cazzo me ne fotte
Se c'avete del denaro?*

(Eh beh?)

A New York

per Annie Lanzilotto e Rose Imparato
(@Small's Jazz Club)

I know I'm a New Yorker
(Why?!)
because
Whenever I behold her skyscrapers,
And Parks,
I'm reminded of the infinite Promise
she sparks
And I know that the skies,
For her, are just an
optimistic beginning,
that's why I scribble lines
with her frantic rhythm in
mind so my guido verse
can shine explicit inspired
by her uptown girl moves
so exquisite . . . .

I know I'm a New Yorker
(How?!)   cuz
When I was in *Firenze*
on a visit,

I made no bones about Where I
was From:

Ro' Bronx!

And I'd say it over again If

they didn't hear it!

I know I'm a New Yorker
(Why?!)
Because the flow Of the *metroplitana* is
much like the blood
flow of my veins

And even if nowadays
New York,
only dines with tourists And
out of towners,
In awe Of her
grandiose tricks,

I still love her
Because her streets
Still teem with best
minds Who aimlessly
crawl down
the   gentrified sidewalks still
fiending for that
angry fix . . . . . .

Guido Poetics

All you Sucker Bards and skeptics,
Premature ejaculators and narcoleptics
Open up your ears while the glint off this
Malocchio gold horn smacks you in the face
as if shit hit the fan, and when things get a little
hectic in this place where are you Sucker
Bards gonna stand if not on some street corner
copping pleas,
shouting demands to the
effect that these Guido
Poetics spit vicious be
put in check:

Locked up in a cage somewhere *magari*
down *a Santo Spirito o ancora meglio*
giù a Union Square?

MA COSA CAZZO PUOI DIRMI
IF I TOLD YOU WHAT MADE UP THIS RHYTHM-LIKE
COMBINAZIONE?

SCIABLACONE,
in bitter tones this guido verse
dethrones you like sly
corleonese blasting mustache
pete in his voice box in
mulberry street tenement with
make shift *rivoltella* that breaks
apart over roof tops *mentre*
young turks *se la filano.*

Ti sbagli di grosso pero if you
think these Guido Poetics are a type
of flow capable only of conjuring
up visions that drift thru the
mind's eye like smoke off a
montecristo that drifts in the air in
front of store front social clubs in
late *ferragosto* down on Belmont
Ave right off of *centottantasette*.

I say this flow blows thru your
banal banter with candor that defames
your legacy and leaves
relatives reticent—

the fact is you can't fuck with this
sentiment that's remnant of *via tasso*
inscriptions—yeah, I said it.

Don't blame me if you're scandalized
Because these guido poetics went off
and set it
Worse than *Crocco e Ninco Nanco*
Whose *brigantaggio* theatrics
were anything but slapstick
and pathetic

Sucker Bard, this verse
*A confronto il tuo, 'si moscio e stanco, Non
sia quello solito d'un saltimbanco*
As a matter of fact:

The secret of these poetics
is fundamental Like

acrobatics and calisthenics

Therefore it's genetic
that this
Guido verse packs static of the
Same aesthetics as South
Brain Tree *processi* that
shocked
the Red Scare epoch tragic

Before you get dramatic Think
twice before you declare that
you've had it up to here with
these *comportamenti anarchici*
filled with loathing and fear
That even puts laurelled poets
in a panic
ovvero una
frenesia
that's manic

Face it Sucker Bards
Your strophes

shatter too easily Under
poetic mass so titanic
You bust your shit on Icebergs
massicci, never slim thus
branding yourselves the biggest
sfigati ever seen on this side of
such a rotten planet, victim of
these guido poetics that upstage
your sucker's hymn, regaling all its
cantors with

knuckle sandwiches
and attacks asthmatic as they saunter off stage befuddled and bruised
all the way up top from rearranged faces down to busted shins,
looking to lay themselves out on adjustable beds craftmatic.

New Haven

Dico: this verse zounds beatified
While I make the past present by
reciting lines electrified
dal tuo sguardo, descendant
di nobiltà kushita as it reigns
benevolent with its vibrant
eyed smile   that summons
up an infinity of sunshine
that smacks
The atmosphere magnificent
despite gray skies that sob
dejected and reticent
above damp
New Haven streets
Where in love we
 Walk hand in hand
Senza scopo

I say this verse zounds beatified
Intensifying this minute, commanding
the day
to stand carelessly still while
pedestrians make way and greater
efforts to get their fill   of your
classical mode as you strode,
fluttering ahead of me *come una
colomba verso il cielo* as if your
soles were caressed
by the air beneath them and lo,

Ti dico this verse zounds beatified

As I sing your feline ways
Ed entro sto pensiero sereno
Sul foglio steso your curves
expound like The arched back
of a Black Cat's silhouette
As it dances languidly
Up a graffiti tattered brick wall
Because if you ask me
Your sweet footsteps even
Got something to do with
A sweet form of anarchy
Whose ecstasy is
Of a vast felicity sparked
By verse that zounds beatified

As I recite brown
eyes
Lit up satisfied so profound
They seem two stars
lingering in countryside
moonlight illuminating that
young adolescent, who
timidly looking toward them
for guidance, passes the
cemetery *mandando su una*
preghiera ai suoi morti,
stramorti
and all the rest

I say this verse zounds beatified as I
take your
hand and bring its softness
to my face, intoxicate myself in its perfume and kiss it
gently just to steal a taste

while I attest That
your angelic
presence
keeps lames glaring dumbfounded Stuck
without even a sentence
Because until you say the word
They remain *stonati* as they
bow down and spit
una corona sana a tutti i santi

Their last miserable attempt
At true penance While
they forever climb
mount
Purgatory You reign in
paradise basking in eternal
eminence.

Sub terrain 6 train Blues

Newsstand full of porno mags
And periodicals, whatever you choose
Scan each cover in search of reason
And an earthly muse
Wet my whistle with Wild Turkey
The night becomes less murky
Must be those Sub terrain 6 train Blues
I mutter to myself
As the harmonica wails to the screeching steel Wheels
of the iron horse.

Georgie boy belts out "Born under a Bad Sign"
John Deer hat tilted low tapping in time on the
Platform in a pair of scuffed Alligator shoes
A real Mozart of makeshift jukeboxes,
And all is right with a bottle of Black Velvet And
a pack of Lucky Strikes
Because that's the taste of a street musician
Who's given his life to those Sub terrain 6 train Blues.

He doesn't dig bling bling or
black limousines just let
him rock the Metro till it Lindy Hops to the next stop because
his music of the masses
uplifts the soul son of
man hustler working a
miracle with a beggar's
tune to Catch a quick
buck as
Riders walk a hurried gait, In
the distance
rumbles The Muse's Call

Sound that pops like dusty vinyl
Always skipping a beat
Who said matters of the heart were neat?
Who said life was all gravy?
There is always a fly in that chicken potpie
And thumbnails in milkshakes that would
make grown men cry. So take a swig of
some Turkey with me, don't be shy Slow
your roll for a while So I can tell you on the
sly that this is a fragile molten ball of clay
that
We stroll upon and the Shylock's
Got us on borrowed time so before the
Whole shithouse goes up in smoke
Spare Georgie a dime
So that rickety-racket jive Doesn't blare
in vain like jukeboxes of cracked up
plastic And rusted chrome in junk house
dives Where every 45 goes round and
round   SNAP! POP! Nonetheless that
sweet Syncopated sound.

Georgie let that harmonica sizzle the
Sub terrain, man sprinkle me with that Muse's
love because it may be   makeshift but your sound
is a space ship, that gives me earfuls of dreams
that are realized.

Joey's Footnote

Joe I found you face down on your
living room floor lifeless body
empty like A bottle of homemade
wine feet gashed on jagged shards
of glass scattered about that black
and white face that faded in a
twilight of forgotten times.

Your passage into the Valley
of Death's Shadow
Didn't go unnoticed and by that
slow *tammurriata* that thumps
softly on that swap meet radio
this poem will be your
farewell funeral dirge

You were a cat that found yourself
obscured in a great forest of
flashbulbs and photo opts where it
was all smoke and mirrors and
politicians rode in Columbus Day
floats with guidette beauty queens
passing the masses, whose English
was tattered with Bronx and
Brooklyn, giving them a good
gander at their perfect almost
plastic pearly whites.

And COME ON BOY!
                    like Louis
bid Sam on "Oh Marie"

let your soul rise 'cuz it
won't go incognito among
slapped Costellos and fat
bastards exclaiming
*That's a spicy Meat-a-
ball!*

Man, shit isn't just
                                    about Sunday dinners Columbus or
Mustache Petes clipped in neighborhood barber shops by young
turks who want their taste.

Peppy you're the *gatto* that
got caught in between the
image war of *la malavita* and
Renaissance plated malaria
mosquito famine infested
memory of town where the
houses were hewn from the
marble mountainside.

You dug the past but didn't
idealize it to the point of myth
that breeds misconception. You
sure as hell were at the far side of
pretension because every man—
peasant *padrino* and
philosopher all deserved equal
attention in the annals of Italian
American lore.

You dug the past and knew that
the future was the only thing that
was really yours.

You would look back with reverence but
were irreverent when old timers always
tried to dictate where you were going
because people like you were sick of
looking up to crooners like Perry Como
when you really wanted to follow Poets
like Miguel Piñero.

Joey you have a place in this
starry night as the guy that
knows reality is to our making
and some of us don't want that
middle class mundane suburb
dinner table scene rather we
rest content with the role of
wanderers that trek the globe
wearing down soles looking for
souls who can spare us some
time to read our wide eyed
Poetry and Prose.

*Giuse' spero che
quest'urlo preghiera ti
tocchi nell'abisso
lontano da ' stu mondo!*

Because I'm here and I
know now that icons are
stuck in written history
void of substance while
those people of the soil
with calloused hands *che
zappavano terra* are as real
and unwritten as a sun

shower in May.

Mentre la volpe
si sposa
I'll remember   you.
I'll remember *nonno*.

And I know that made history
will light my way but unmade
history is my square slab of
marble from the quarry to be
sculpted in my fashion.

Dawn's sky runs red and in the
memory of your death the shards
are swept away, the photo in my
breast pocket because gilded
frames and rusted nails couldn't
contain the story of a man who
was a real bird of passage.

XTC

I feel the Love all through my spine. I feel it
in the glances of every smiling face, in every
pound given.

The drum's energy, every
insecurity hidden. A kiss is a
journey Come ride this,
kitten. Tongue all down her
throat, to the music bodies
float.

I'm seeking the goddess of this Rave.

Fell into the light and awoke in a valley
of Break Beats, The DJ was King, and
the mood was just right, but who held
the stare of that Heavenly Vision
bouncing in rhythm to the flash of the
strobe light?

After September 11th

We roll thru the streets
of Manhattan losing our
sanity.

Because New York feels dead, a
massive end to its cacophonous
reality.

Phantasmal melancholy sky
scrapers kiss the skies goodbye

as
We drive thru Manhattan looking for
dolls that wear their tattered hearts
on their sleeves.

Billy Joel blasts on speakers, and they say
a tree grows in Brooklyn but my heart is an
empty seed.

Inhale\exhale My
Open Mind is
numb and my
Broken Heart is
frail.

We glide thru the streets like satin curtains that
sail thru winds that brush my face making me
know that my soul, though filled with sin, will
reach The Bronx by morning light.

May I reach The Bronx by morning light, or I'll walk
on the East River and fade from sight.

This world will spin, stop it might but
I'll cruise the Manhattan alleys.

This cat can't reach newer heights.
And the cat next to me is looking to smoke.

Driver looks on, eyes
brimming with hope.

His muse is out there.
If the skies fall I'll cope.

If angels call,
I'll climb to Heaven on
a velvet rope.

And if I reach the Pearly Gates I bet
they'll be closed, I won't blame St
Peter, I'm always late; besides my
fate awaits a later date, and this
wood and haze has given me a
mental earthquake.

So I come on down, but
not to Bob Barker.

This eerie doo-wop ballad
confounds me, as I look
out the window beholding
this bugged out
streetwalker.

It astounds me how we swing on
shoestrings never expecting to
come tumbling down.

I'm coming on down, but
not to Bob Barker.

To me the price is never right,
maybe it's because I'm a New
Yorker.

Spiritual Crisis

To me Spirituality was never kind.
Tried to be Muslim but I'm too much
a glutton for smoked swine and
guzzled gallons of basement wine.

Baptized a Catholic so
They say I'm fine,
But I can't get past the Fact
that gold plated crucifixes and
cannibalism can be Divine.

My mentality once was
Buddhist, to crush desire And
achieve Nirvana.
To be still as the moon while   A
river of headlights flows Below
me.

But contemplation takes Too
long.
My journey is for people to Know
me.

And in the eye of the Crisis, stuck in
this spiritual revolving door Drowned
in dizziness I finally saw that
fulfillment was to be found in the
Muse's song, like stormy
weather and blaring horns, that jar you awake
on an early crimson morn sending you out to
those 6AM insomniac   streets

in search of fertile fields of the mind to plant your corn
that will nourish souls and devils scorn.

Just a thought and a poem is born By
the soft strum of that damsel's
Dulcimer that mends souls torn.

So whenever I feel lost I
Utter a couple of end-lined
Rhymes requesting my

Lady of Abundance and She'll
appear at my side And nourish
me spiritually
with her poetic fruit.

Maddalena

Mystic Mistress with your witch like ways
Casting spells of natural voodoo that make
Hobos ask Oracles from whence ye came,
Whenever they see you walk the marketplace
Lanes, a goddess, amidst metropolitan gridlock
And melancholy drunken Danes who lust all
Day after those bread line lips that keep them Waiting
forever to taste sweet juices of Sensuousness like
Panettone dipped in Amaretto.

And they all chat in tune with the tapping
Of your stilettos to concrete jungle floor,
Asking each other if they know of a cure
That can render them clean and sober so they can lie
Next to you at night warmed up by your shapely Shell
that smells of cinnamon and honeydew.

Broken cardboard boxes are their mattresses on bed
Frame of cement steps in

Christ the Scientist doorways but they're too hopped
up on love to realize they lie blanketed by the
suffocating shadow of looming lonely scaffold that
shields them from the uncaring elements
Ambivalently aspiring to find your foxy silhouette dotted Up in
some far out fantastic constellation that borders the edge Of this
gone galaxy.

Hips hypnotize moving side to side In
your cat walk strut.
Shining supple thighs thunder

In those eggplant leather pants
And I know you mean no
Harm to those other birds
With green eyes just because
Amidst the discarded aluminum
Cans and shredded week old
Newspapers its all Christmas
Ornaments and confetti when You
walk on by.

So they can hate while
Street musicians in Grand Central
Station compose the ballad
Of a girl that can outshine Times
Square on New Year's Eve with the
Bounce of her sable curls and
White gold bracelets, that adorn
Each delicate wrist, from Tiffany's

French manicured nails and fragrance,
whose name escapes me, lingers with their
senses long after you leave them in a serene
stupor.

The streets are your admirers and you feign
Not to know of it and that's what makes Your
style classy but not flashy.

And when you're done enchanting heads for The
night you come home to lavish
Central Park West abode greeting that
Poet playing janitor in his 4 to 6 graveyard
Shift mopping the lobby floor so your reflection Can
out sparkle the granite's shiny hue.

He says hello and asks what's new
And you reply you're off to jet set out
West and cannot wait to sizzle and tease
the pimps that scout Filmore street in
the City of The Golden Gate.

Those cats are in for a surprise because the Only
thing worth your magic is love.

La nubiana ritrovata . . . .

E quella a me: <<Nessun maggior dolore
che ricordarsi del tempo felice ne la
miseria; e ciò sa 'l tuo dottor.

Ma s'a conoscer la prima radice del
nostro amor tu hai contanto affetto
Dirò come colui che piange e dice.>>
Dante, *Inferno*, canto v:121-126
O donna formosa With her glance,
reminiscent of black kittens
kissed by the soft light of a full red
moon in the intimate breezy mid-
summer stillness:

the first time I seen her in grand
central station my glance got
stuck in some sort of
physically spiritual infatuation;

as if,
weaving thru come and go masses,
she descended from Athena's
far out glistening constellation with her
smile like blackout accentuated skies
with planetary vibrations and her eyes
that remind cats of lunar eclipses and
super novae
that explode in harbinger jubilation

because from the moment I heard
her speak *già sapevo* that

her cadence stretched back
to egyptian hieroglyphics— like
 radiant depictions of *Iside* on
pyramid walls along with Horus and
Osiro
so
it's no wonder why
 I aspire to craft these lines
to be incised Majestic
on the sides of obelisks which stand
in glorious testament To the
intrinsically syncopated melody
which encompassed her soul
sublime and beatific, a unification of
the cosmic dynamo *tutto stellato*
over a sordid little imperfect world *farabutto
intossicato*

Kind of like that
rapid fire bop riff
blown exquisite
whose   languid
sound permeates
west 44th street:

She's the embodiment of BIRD LIVES!
Basking in a sweet style futurist eternity!!

And with emotions running
highly combustible her red
velvet locks, tinted by the
flames of Apollo's chariot ,
would even undulate
si vibrante che pure

quando si incazzava
colpiva sempre a centro
con immensità—ti giuro!

il fatto è che
to be next to her   *un*
minuto
was worth *un attimo*
 nei cieli co' i santi—di sicuro!   *un anno senza lei*
è pieno inferno—te lo giuro
that leaves you like an empty *damigiana*
stored away *giù in cantina*
Come next September— *porca*
puttana

confuso like *some johnny come*
marcovaldo harvesting mushrooms
off some marciapiede nel
milanese . . . because *la vita in*
montagna he remembers

frate', ottuso cioé ngrippat worse than Ovidio who, in
solemn meter meant to rehearse qualche racconto
sfondante of arms, war, and violence che ogni volta I try
to capture such fare, in intimate silence, cioé the fleeting
hands of time to contort broken verse into epic tales of
blood sport,   forged to the maddening clash of a samnite's
gladius against the clamorous thrash of a thracian's
trident— coupled with the masses that roar maniacally
astounded—

 my nubian muse
plays captor to my
inward eye and with

my strophes that sear
the heart, with similes
of fire, and cupid's
darts do their part,

perciò I can't do
nientaltrochè
frame her delectable essence
in endless flight

she's Daphne ,
defiant of Apollo's
amorous advances,
and beseeching her father repeatedly

in un alloro si trasmutò and became the
stuff which coined the phrase "*poeti
laureati*" and this broken verse begins to
flow from Golden Age antiquity to this
mundane here and now horror show go
fuck yourself ubiquity

*and my attempt is to convert
emozioni dolorose* into a vast
ethereal felicity *perciò vi
racconto gone momenti* of an
utter timeless rapture with
metaphors that become that
coccinella resting on your
shoulder, *mentre ti scrocchi
qualche fico di nascosto*,

which summon up
symphonies of *raggi*

di sole
brillanti in pieno,

sdraiati in quel
posto sotto
l'ombra
d'un cespuglio in Central Park

like a spark nascosto
dietro nubi notturne di
seta out over some falò
on plebeian white sands
sul mar tirreno con varie
sfumature di un buio
roseo sublime
infine
that wondrous
token of her hourglass silhouette vastly accentuated by the
light that *sottilmente* filters thru the dark inner regions of a
gone mentality . . . thumping an archaic rhythm that zounds an
atavistic insanity of *tammurri* and base drums with that
honeyed *chitarra* playing this wild *pizzicata brigantesca* that
breaks the breath taking
bourbon binge filled lull realization

where recalling past times of ephemeral bliss
in this evermore present abyss equals infernal bitterness

(e ciò sa 'l tuo dottor)

Let his poem echo *in piazza*
'round midnight To the gone
bass-line of this love supreme
mood, Wrapped in a melancholic

prism,
Whose spectrum stretches the
Panoramic horizons of my lonely as a cloud wandering memory,

she appears rivissuta
ceremoniously

O nubiana ritrovata Dressed
in crimson tinged immaculate
& regal:

And lackadaisically Day Dreams, of
accompanying Her *fino al* New
Haven-line *binario*, conjure up a star
crossed lover *scenario* and before she
departs

Embracing her tight, *stracolmo*
of some of that
quinto cerchio disio

kissing her deeply,
a part of my soul
dies, like tears
caressing cheeks,
as they befell the eyes of *Didone*
as she lay there bleeding,

and with a cadence *tipo*
una *colomba*
in fuga

soavamente
I bid her a *bitter*
sweet *Addio.*

Guido Haiku

This bop riff baffles cats
endlessly thru mid day
giving birth to verse.

Pazzo sto fatto that I can flip
verse two ways: *In italiano* Or
in slick guido bronxese.

Boom bap befuddles down
stairs neighbor as she walks
her pup aimlessly.

Auguri a te cara mamma
plays on the radio and
blasts *Rosaria Bianchi* in
the damp mid-day sad air.

Bombardiers flying
Overhead off of bass plucked Insane
by Sam Jones.

Autumn tree branches
Nude in the gray horizon Tomato
plants uprooted.

Venetian blinds drawn
Down dejected in sadness Brown
skin lady lost.

The six train ghostly
Screeches down the tunnel wrought With
a sense of rhyme.

Jazz Man blow your heart
Endlessly, hold a soft note Like
a deep kiss grand.

Silky skin soft to
Naked touch like cocoa butter Your
scent I bask in.

Mayday came and we
Met again after 3 years Laugh
now, cry later.

Dry turkey scraps
In a silver *vassoio*
Reaches table's end.

La Resistenza

I already told you motherfuckers:
My verse is like a *strega's* curse so *brutti
figli di quella troia di tua madre* instead
of sending you to mass so you can just
extort wads of cash from sheepish
Monsignors who acquiesce
 marauding black shirted bastard squads

 insomma vi manda sei piedi sotto— Tucked
away in some *montanaro* landscape
reminiscent of how they did Bogart in
Treasure of the Sierra Madre *Comunque sia!
Cazzo me ne fotto*!!

 fuck your whole centro sociale

and don't try to act like
your   poets   are
descendant of dominant
co-opted futurist
velocity that left
F.T.,
(From the depth of a
ditch) with such an
exquisite swift
epiphany to pitch the
rhapsodic frame work
for a flash mechanical
shift manifesto over
one score ago on the
window of his skull

which , in this verse,
is devastatingly prevalent

and it shows that Your
flaccid minded *blocco
studentesco* can't
withstand My strict
regiment of *toro
scatenato* calisthenics
that crosses the border
of Your
State of Provinciality
da clandestino thus it
causes disorder cuz
It's got this militant mentality

Tipo arlecchino:

Carlo and his friendly game
Of baseball bat wielding
Sindacalists smacked the shit
out of *lavoro nero camice
nere* grandfathers with
unmitigated brutality in
Our Lady of Pompeii basements

Anzi it's More like that
specific time some house
Of savoy monarch got his
wig pushed
Back

(*tutto meschino!*)

by some Greasy
haired wide-
eyed street
anarchist by way
of Paterson,
 New Jersey,

In hope of superbly
going Down in a hail of
stomps Meted out by
Caramba amidst
Rebellious scene of
regicide reality!

And yeah Benito may have
been from a family of
Anarchists
 but his ideas developed
into the farcical fruition
of broken
risorgimento ideals

That easily galvanized illiterate
bracciante masses with its
tragically comedic 20th century
interpretation of antiquity while
it cooked up plots to conquer
Ethiopia to save face from that
figuraccia Menelik II *ha fatto*
combina' ai bisnonni . . .

so let these strophes
with their *incendiario*
boplicitic flames

dissipate any idiocy you
disperse
into the carbon
dioxide saturated
atmosphere
 egregiously

So recite your rhymes and try to bite
Some of Rino's freshest lines

(*SCEMO, I VERSI DI RINO NON SI SCROCCANO!*)

Let this be my antithetical anthem
That deflates your get   gassed
braggadocio
Rhymes like the tires on your black
Alfa Romeo and scratches on the
driver side *sportello* a black cat of
sabotage
which symbolizes
cover of darkness *bordello*

Thus let me take a strophe to poetize
About the opaque cat-like eyes of
Carthaginian Monarch that
epitomized the Mediterranean For its
odysseys
And cultural cross pollination
That gave birth to nations of
varie sfumature di colori And
the realization that civilization
is eternally Caught up in the
flux, you foolishly pertain to
contain in your puerile growth

spurts
Of *turboismo giù in piazza*

You get stupid with
leftist masses With
your stiff upper lips
and your heads
All *pelati*
Rocking
Black
Puma sweat suits and
puffing your bird chests
out you *babbioni sfigati*
become caricatures of
pachucos   posted up on
Santa Monica Blvd. or just
a bunch of *ciccioni
balordosi* that act hard
when they're all *zozzosi
pe' mezz' 'a folla*

with the pigs
on their side

but when it gets dark
you are just   some
poor boy black
shirted marks
with nowhere to hide—

who get run up on by red and black anarchists who spray paint
        across your *sede's* Facade:

Acknowledgments

Earlier versions of the listed poems have been previously published by the following outlets:

"Mondrayork." Palabras Luminosas/Luminous Words. New York: Rogue Scholars Press, 2016, pp. 6; 109-110.

"Stoop Dub." Ovunque Siamo: New Italian American Writing. Vol. 1 Num. 1. 2015. https://ovunquesiamoweb.com/archive/current-issue-vol-1-no-1/angelo-zeolla/

"New Haven." Philadelphia Poets 2015. Vol. 21 Philadelphia: Philadelphia Poets, 2015, pp. 74-76.

"Crazy Annie." Philadelphia Poets 2014. Vol.20 Philadelphia: Philadelphia Poets, 2014, pp. 42-43.

"Joey's Footnote" Philadelphia Poets 2008. Vol. 14 Philadelphia: Philadelphia Poets, 2008, pp. 72-75.

"Pezzo da Novanta." Avanti Popolo: Italian-American Writers Sail Beyond Columbus. San Francisco: Manic D Press, 2008, pp. 46-55.

The line "I know I'm a New Yorker" contained in "A New York," originates from the poem "Anxiety at Sunset" published in Annie Rachele Lanzillotto's collection of poems, *Schistsong*, Bordighera Press, 2013. pp. 78-80.

About the Author

The poet, ANGELO ZEOLLA, was born in the Pelham Bay section of The Bronx, a borough of the City of New York, in 1979. He has a B.A. in Italian Studies and Philosophy from CUNY Queens College and an M.A. from Middlebury College, in 20th Century Italian Literature.

His poetry reflects his background as the child of Italian immigrants, as well as it is informed by his having had to navigate through two different worlds—that of his Italian origins, with that of, the neighborhood of his birth, in The Bronx: The former being italofone, provincial, as well connected to the earth in a Silonian sense, and the latter being anglofone, hyphenated, in flux and ambivalent to the old world, yet aggressively protective of any encroachment to an Italian American identity from any perceived threat.

His poems are a byproduct of trying to make sense of all this, and ultimately a realization of the solidarity that the poet uncovers in capturing the essence of humanity's daily-multilayered existence.

VIA Folios
A refereed book series dedicated to the culture of Italians and Italian Americans.

NICHOLAS A. DiCHARIO. *Giovanni's Tree*. Vol. 161. Literature.
ADELE ANNESI. *What She Takes Away*. Vol. 160. Novel.
ANNIE RACHELE LANZILLOTTO. *Whaddyacall the Wind?*. Vol. 159. Memoir.
JULIA LISELLA. *Our Lively Kingdom*. Vol. 158. Poetry.
MARK CIABATTARI. *When the Mask Slips*. Vol. 157. Novel.
JENNIFER MARTELLI. *The Queen of Queens*. Vol. 156. Poetry.
TONY TADDEI. *The Sons of the Santorelli*. Vol. 155. Literature.
FRANCO RICCI. *Preston Street • Corso Italias*. Vol. 154. History.
MIKE FIORITO. *The Hated Ones*. Vol. 153. Literature.
PATRICIA DUNN. *Last Stop on the 6*. Vol. 152. Novel.
WILLIAM BOELHOWER. *Immigrant Autobiography*. Vol. 151. Literary Criticism.
MARC DIPAOLO. *Fake Italian*. Vol. 150. Literature.
GAIL REITANO. *Italian Love Cake*. Vol. 149. Novel.
VINCENT PANELLA. *Sicilian Dreams*. Vol. 148. Novel.
MARK CIABATTARI. *The Literal Truth: Rizzoli Dreams of Eating the Apple of Earthly Delights*. Vol. 147. Novel.
MARK CIABATTARI. *Dreams of An Imaginary New Yorker Named Rizzoli*. Vol. 146. Novel.
LAURETTE FOLK. *The End of Aphrodite*. Vol. 145. Novel.
ANNA CITRINO. *A Space Between*. Vol. 144. Poetry
MARIA FAMÀ. *The Good for the Good*. Vol. 143. Poetry.
ROSEMARY CAPPELLO. *Wonderful Disaster*. Vol. 142. Poetry.
B. AMORE. *Journeys on the Wheel*. Vol. 141. Poetry.
ALDO PALAZZESCHI. *The Manifestos of Aldo Palazzeschi*. Vol 140. Literature.
ROSS TALARICO. *The Reckoning*. Vol 139. Poetry.
MICHELLE REALE. *Season of Subtraction*. Vol 138. Poetry.
MARISA FRASCA. *Wild Fennel*. Vol 137. Poetry.
RITA ESPOSITO WATSON. *Italian Kisses*. Vol. 136. Memoir.
SARA FRUNER. *Bitter Bites from Sugar Hills*. Vol. 135. Poetry.
KATHY CURTO. *Not for Nothing*. Vol. 134. Memoir.
JENNIFER MARTELLI. *My Tarantella*. Vol. 133. Poetry.
MARIA TERRONE. *At Home in the New World*. Vol. 132. Essays.
GIL FAGIANI. *Missing Madonnas*. Vol. 131. Poetry.
LEWIS TURCO. *The Sonnetarium*. Vol. 130. Poetry.
JOE AMATO. *Samuel Taylor's Hollywood Adventure*. Vol. 129. Novel.
BEA TUSIANI. *Con Amore*. Vol. 128. Memoir.
MARIA GIURA. *What My Father Taught Me*. Vol. 127. Poetry.
STANISLAO PUGLIESE. *A Century of Sinatra*. Vol. 126. Popular Culture.
TONY ARDIZZONE. *The Arab's Ox*. Vol. 125. Novel.
PHYLLIS CAPELLO. *Packs Small Plays Big*. Vol. 124. Literature.
FRED GARDAPHÉ. *Read 'em and Reap*. Vol. 123. Criticism.
JOSEPH A. AMATO. *Diagnostics*. Vol 122. Literature.
DENNIS BARONE. *Second Thoughts*. Vol 121. Poetry.

OLIVIA K. CERRONE. *The Hunger Saint.* Vol 120. Novella.
GARIBLADI M. LAPOLLA. *Miss Rollins in Love.* Vol 119. Novel.
JOSEPH TUSIANI. *A Clarion Call.* Vol 118. Poetry.
JOSEPH A. AMATO. *My Three Sicilies.* Vol 117. Poetry & Prose.
MARGHERITA COSTA. *Voice of a Virtuosa and Coutesan.* Vol 116. Poetry.
NICOLE SANTALUCIA. *Because I Did Not Die.* Vol 115. Poetry.
MARK CIABATTARI. *Preludes to History.* Vol 114. Poetry.
HELEN BAROLINI. *Visits.* Vol 113. Novel.
ERNESTO LIVORNI. *The Fathers' America.* Vol 112. Poetry.
MARIO B. MIGNONE. *The Story of My People.* Vol 111. Non-fiction.
GEORGE GUIDA. *The Sleeping Gulf.* Vol 110. Poetry.
JOEY NICOLETTI. *Reverse Graffiti.* Vol 109. Poetry.
GIOSE RIMANELLI. *Il mestiere del furbo.* Vol 108. Criticism.
LEWIS TURCO. *The Hero Enkidu.* Vol 107. Poetry.
AL TACCONELLI. *Perhaps Fly.* Vol 106. Poetry.
RACHEL GUIDO DEVRIES. *A Woman Unknown in Her Bones.* Vol 105. Poetry.
BERNARD BRUNO. *A Tear and a Tear in My Heart.* Vol 104. Non-fiction.
FELIX STEFANILE. *Songs of the Sparrow.* Vol 103. Poetry.
FRANK POLIZZI. *A New Life with Bianca.* Vol 102. Poetry.
GIL FAGIANI. *Stone Walls.* Vol 101. Poetry.
LOUISE DESALVO. *Casting Off.* Vol 100. Fiction.
MARY JO BONA. *I Stop Waiting for You.* Vol 99. Poetry.
RACHEL GUIDO DEVRIES. *Stati zitt, Josie.* Vol 98. Children's Literature. $8
GRACE CAVALIERI. *The Mandate of Heaven.* Vol 97. Poetry.
MARISA FRASCA. *Via incanto.* Vol 96. Poetry.
DOUGLAS GLADSTONE. *Carving a Niche for Himself.* Vol 95. History.
MARIA TERRONE. *Eye to Eye.* Vol 94. Poetry.
CONSTANCE SANCETTA. *Here in Cerchio.* Vol 93. Local History.
MARIA MAZZIOTTI GILLAN. *Ancestors' Song.* Vol 92. Poetry.
MICHAEL PARENTI. *Waiting for Yesterday: Pages from a Street Kid's Life.* Vol 90. Memoir.
ANNIE LANZILLOTTO. *Schistsong.* Vol 89. Poetry.
EMANUEL DI PASQUALE. *Love Lines.* Vol 88. Poetry.
CAROSONE & LOGIUDICE. *Our Naked Lives.* Vol 87. Essays.
JAMES PERICONI. *Strangers in a Strange Land: A Survey of Italian-Language American Books.* Vol 86. Book History.
DANIELA GIOSEFFI. *Escaping La Vita Della Cucina.* Vol 85. Essays.
MARIA FAMÀ. *Mystics in the Family.* Vol 84. Poetry.
ROSSANA DEL ZIO. *From Bread and Tomatoes to Zuppa di Pesce "Ciambotto".* Vol. 83. Memoir.
LORENZO DELBOCA. *Polentoni.* Vol 82. Italian Studies.
SAMUEL GHELLI. *A Reference Grammar.* Vol 81. Italian Language.
ROSS TALARICO. *Sled Run.* Vol 80. Fiction.
FRED MISURELLA. *Only Sons.* Vol 79. Fiction.
FRANK LENTRICCHIA. *The Portable Lentricchia.* Vol 78. Fiction.
RICHARD VETERE. *The Other Colors in a Snow Storm.* Vol 77. Poetry.

GARIBALDI LAPOLLA. *Fire in the Flesh*. Vol 76 Fiction & Criticism.
GEORGE GUIDA. *The Pope Stories*. Vol 75 Prose.
ROBERT VISCUSI. *Ellis Island*. Vol 74. Poetry.
ELENA GIANINI BELOTTI. *The Bitter Taste of Strangers Bread*. Vol 73. Fiction.
PINO APRILE. *Terroni*. Vol 72. Italian Studies.
EMANUEL DI PASQUALE. *Harvest*. Vol 71. Poetry.
ROBERT ZWEIG. *Return to Naples*. Vol 70. Memoir.
AIROS & CAPPELLI. *Guido*. Vol 69. Italian/American Studies.
FRED GARDAPHÉ. *Moustache Pete is Dead! Long Live Moustache Pete!*. Vol 67. Literature/Oral History.
PAOLO RUFFILLI. *Dark Room/Camera oscura*. Vol 66. Poetry.
HELEN BAROLINI. *Crossing the Alps*. Vol 65. Fiction.
COSMO FERRARA. *Profiles of Italian Americans*. Vol 64. Italian Americana.
GIL FAGIANI. *Chianti in Connecticut*. Vol 63. Poetry.
BASSETTI & D'ACQUINO. *Italic Lessons*. Vol 62. Italian/American Studies.
CAVALIERI & PASCARELLI, Eds. *The Poet's Cookbook*. Vol 61. Poetry/Recipes.
EMANUEL DI PASQUALE. *Siciliana*. Vol 60. Poetry.
NATALIA COSTA, Ed. *Bufalini*. Vol 59. Poetry.
RICHARD VETERE. *Baroque*. Vol 58. Fiction.
LEWIS TURCO. *La Famiglia/The Family*. Vol 57. Memoir.
NICK JAMES MILETI. *The Unscrupulous*. Vol 56. Humanities.
BASSETTI. ACCOLLA. D'AQUINO. *Italici: An Encounter with Piero Bassetti*. Vol 55. Italian Studies.
GIOSE RIMANELLI. *The Three-legged One*. Vol 54. Fiction.
CHARLES KLOPP. *Bele Antiche Stòrie*. Vol 53. Criticism.
JOSEPH RICAPITO. *Second Wave*. Vol 52. Poetry.
GARY MORMINO. *Italians in Florida*. Vol 51. History.
GIANFRANCO ANGELUCCI. *Federico F*. Vol 50. Fiction.
ANTHONY VALERIO. *The Little Sailor*. Vol 49. Memoir.
ROSS TALARICO. *The Reptilian Interludes*. Vol 48. Poetry.
RACHEL GUIDO DE VRIES. *Teeny Tiny Tino's Fishing Story*. Vol 47. Children's Literature.
EMANUEL DI PASQUALE. *Writing Anew*. Vol 46. Poetry.
MARIA FAMÀ. *Looking For Cover*. Vol 45. Poetry.
ANTHONY VALERIO. *Toni Cade Bambara's One Sicilian Night*. Vol 44. Poetry.
EMANUEL CARNEVALI. *Furnished Rooms*. Vol 43. Poetry.
BRENT ADKINS. et al., Ed. *Shifting Borders. Negotiating Places*. Vol 42. Conference.
GEORGE GUIDA. *Low Italian*. Vol 41. Poetry.
GARDAPHÈ, GIORDANO, TAMBURRI. *Introducing Italian Americana*. Vol 40. Italian/American Studies.
DANIELA GIOSEFFI. *Blood Autumn/Autunno di sangue*. Vol 39. Poetry.
FRED MISURELLA. *Lies to Live By*. Vol 38. Stories.
STEVEN BELLUSCIO. *Constructing a Bibliography*. Vol 37. Italian Americana.
ANTHONY JULIAN TAMBURRI, Ed. *Italian Cultural Studies 2002*. Vol 36. Essays.

BEA TUSIANI. *con amore*. Vol 35. Memoir.
FLAVIA BRIZIO-SKOV, Ed. *Reconstructing Societies in the Aftermath of War*.
   Vol 34. History.
TAMBURRI. et al., Eds. *Italian Cultural Studies 2001*. Vol 33. Essays.
ELIZABETH G. MESSINA, Ed. *In Our Own Voices*.
   Vol 32. Italian/American Studies.
STANISLAO G. PUGLIESE. *Desperate Inscriptions*. Vol 31. History.
HOSTERT & TAMBURRI, Eds. *Screening Ethnicity*.
   Vol 30. Italian/American Culture.
G. PARATI & B. LAWTON, Eds. *Italian Cultural Studies*. Vol 29. Essays.
HELEN BAROLINI. *More Italian Hours*. Vol 28. Fiction.
FRANCO NASI, Ed. *Intorno alla Via Emilia*. Vol 27. Culture.
ARTHUR L. CLEMENTS. *The Book of Madness & Love*. Vol 26. Poetry.
JOHN CASEY, et al. *Imagining Humanity*. Vol 25. Interdisciplinary Studies.
ROBERT LIMA. *Sardinia/Sardegna*. Vol 24. Poetry.
DANIELA GIOSEFFI. *Going On*. Vol 23. Poetry.
ROSS TALARICO. *The Journey Home*. Vol 22. Poetry.
EMANUEL DI PASQUALE. *The Silver Lake Love Poems*. Vol 21. Poetry.
JOSEPH TUSIANI. *Ethnicity*. Vol 20. Poetry.
JENNIFER LAGIER. *Second Class Citizen*. Vol 19. Poetry.
FELIX STEFANILE. *The Country of Absence*. Vol 18. Poetry.
PHILIP CANNISTRARO. *Blackshirts*. Vol 17. History.
LUIGI RUSTICHELLI, Ed. *Seminario sul racconto*. Vol 16. Narrative.
LEWIS TURCO. *Shaking the Family Tree*. Vol 15. Memoirs.
LUIGI RUSTICHELLI, Ed. *Seminario sulla drammaturgia*.
   Vol 14. Theater/Essays.
FRED GARDAPHÈ. *Moustache Pete is Dead! Long Live Moustache Pete!*.
   Vol 13. Oral Literature.
JONE GAILLARD CORSI. *Il libretto d'autore. 1860 - 1930*. Vol 12. Criticism.
HELEN BAROLINI. *Chiaroscuro: Essays of Identity*. Vol 11. Essays.
PICARAZZI & FEINSTEIN, Eds. *An African Harlequin in Milan*.
   Vol 10. Theater/Essays.
JOSEPH RICAPITO. *Florentine Streets & Other Poems*. Vol 9. Poetry.
FRED MISURELLA. *Short Time*. Vol 8. Novella.
NED CONDINI. *Quartettsatz*. Vol 7. Poetry.
ANTHONY JULIAN TAMBURRI, Ed. *Fuori: Essays by Italian/American
   Lesbiansand Gays*. Vol 6. Essays.
ANTONIO GRAMSCI. P. Verdicchio. Trans. & Intro. *The Southern Question*.
   Vol 5. Social Criticism.
DANIELA GIOSEFFI. *Word Wounds & Water Flowers*. Vol 4. Poetry. $8
WILEY FEINSTEIN. *Humility's Deceit: Calvino Reading Ariosto Reading Calvino*.
   Vol 3. Criticism.
PAOLO A. GIORDANO, Ed. *Joseph Tusiani: Poet. Translator. Humanist*.
   Vol 2. Criticism.
ROBERT VISCUSI. *Oration Upon the Most Recent Death of Christopher Columbus*.
   Vol 1. Poetry.

www.ingramcontent.com/pod-product-compliance
Lightning Source LLC
Chambersburg PA
CBHW022118090426
42743CB00008B/899